Hurry Up

Alan

Illustrated by

A Harcourt Achieve Imprint

www.Rigby.com
1-800-531-5015

Hippo gets his sock.
Hurry up, Hippo!

3

Hippo gets his cap.
Hurry up, Hippo!

4

Hippo gets his glove.
Hurry up, Hippo!

Hippo gets his snack!
Hurry up, Hippo!

Hippo gets his helmet.
Hurry up, Hippo!

11

Hippo gets his bat.
Hurry up, Hippo!

Hippo gets a hit!
Hurry up, Hippo!

Hippo gets a home run!